Letters to My Son

This Book Is For

____

Lots of Love
Always & Forever

____

To My Son

Date: ________

To My Son

Date: ________

To My Son

Date: ________

To My Son

Date:

To My Son

Date: ______

To My Son

Date: ______

To My Son

Date: ________

To My Son

Date:

To My Son

Date: ________

To My Son Date: ________

To My Son

Date: ______

To My Son

Date: ________

To My Son

Date: ________

To My Son

Date: ________

To My Son

Date: ________

To My Son

Date: ________

To My Son

Date: ________

To My Son

Date: ____________

To My Son

Date: ________

To My Son

Date: ________

To My Son

Date:

To My Son

Date: ______

To My Son

Date: ________

To My Son

Date: ________

To My Son

Date: ________

To My Son

Date: ______

To My Son

Date: ________

To My Son

Date: ________

To My Son

Date: ________

To My Son Date: ________

To My Son

Date: ________

To My Son

Date: ______

To My Son

Date: ________

To My Son

Date: ______

To My Son

Date: ____________

To My Son Date: ________

To My Son

Date:

To My Son

Date: ______

To My Son

Date: ________

To My Son

Date: ________

To My Son

Date: ________

To My Son

Date: ________

To My Son

Date: ________

To My Son

Date: ________

To My Son

Date: ____________

To My Son

Date: ____________

To My Son

Date: ________

To My Son

Date: ________

To My Son

Date: ________

To My Son

Date: ______

To My Son

Date: ________

To My Son

Date:

To My Son

Date: ________

To My Son

Date:

To My Son

Date:

To My Son

Date:

To My Son Date: ________

To My Son

Date:

To My Son

Date: ________

To My Son

Date: ______

To My Son

Date: ________

To My Son

Date: ________

To My Son

Date: ________

To My Son

Date:

To My Son

Date: ________

To My Son

Date: ____________

To My Son

Date: ____________

To My Son

Date: ________

To My Son

Date: ________

To My Son

Date: ____________

To My Son

Date: ________

To My Son

Date: ________

To My Son

Date: ______

To My Son

Date: ________

To My Son

Date: ________

To My Son

Date:

To My Son

Date: ________

To My Son

Date: ____________

To My Son

Date: ________

To My Son

Date: ________

To My Son

Date: ________

To My Son

Date: __________

To My Son

Date: ________

To My Son

Date:

To My Son

Date: ________

To My Son

Date: ________

To My Son

Date: ________

To My Son

Date: ____________

To My Son

Date: ________

To My Son

Date: ________

To My Son

Date: ________

To My Son

Date: ________

To My Son

Date: ________

To My Son

Date: ______

To My Son

Date: ________

To My Son

Date: ____

To My Son

Date: ________

To My Son

Date:

To My Son

Date: ________

To My Son

Date: ________

To My Son

Date: ________

To My Son

Date: ____________

To My Son

Date: ________

To My Son

Date: ________

To My Son

Date: ________

To My Son

Date: ________

To My Son Date: ________

To My Son

Date:

To My Son

Date: ________

To My Son

Date: ________

To My Son

Date: ________

To My Son

Date: ______

To My Son

Date: ________

To My Son

Date: ________

To My Son

Date: ________

To My Son

Date: ________

To My Son

Date: ______

To My Son

Date: ______

To My Son

Date: ________

To My Son

Date:

To My Son

Date: ________

To My Son

Date:

To My Son

Date: ________

Made in United States
North Haven, CT
05 June 2025

69508981R00070